Twenty to Make
Knitted
Baby Bootees

Val Pierce

Search Press

First published in Great Britain 2011

Search Press Limited
Wellwood, North Farm Road,
Tunbridge Wells, Kent TN2 3DR

Text copyright © Val Pierce 2011

Photographs by Debbie Patterson at
Search Press Studios

Photographs and design copyright
© Search Press Ltd 2011

ISBN: 978-1-84448-641-0

Suppliers

If you have difficulty in obtaining any of the
materials and equipment mentioned in this book,
then please visit the Search Press website for
details of suppliers: www.searchpress.com

*I dedicate this book to newborn babies
everywhere. May their tiny toes enjoy the
warmth and comfort that these lovingly
knitted bootees will bring!*

Abbreviations:
beg = beginning
cont = continue
dec = decrease
GS = garter stitch (every row knit)
inc = increase
K = knit
LH = left hand
m = make
MB = make bobble (see page 6)
P = purl
psso = pass slipped stitch over
rem = remaining
rep = repeat
RH = right hand
RS = right side
sl = slip stitch
SS = stocking stitch (alternate purl and
  knit rows)
st(s) = stitch(es)
tbl = through the back loop(s)
tog = together
WS = wrong side
yfwd = yarn forward

UK and US terminology:

UK	US
cast off	bind off
moss stitch	seed stitch
stocking stitch	stockinette stitch
yarn forward	yarn over

Printed in Malaysia

Contents

Introduction

The announcement of a new baby never fails to generate excitement in any family. Aunts, cousins, mothers and grandparents all reach for the knitting needles and cannot wait to begin creating something special for the tiny newborn. Irresistibly cute and quick to make, bootees have proved to be a welcome gift for generations; with this in mind, I have designed twenty pairs of adorable little bootees for you to choose from. They range from traditional lacy designs, cute tiny duckling slippers, little strawberry-inspired bootees, trendy fluffy boots and a range of more sturdy-looking knitted boots especially for baby boys!

Each design takes just one ball of yarn or less, and many can be made from the odds and ends left over in your stash. Novice knitters will be able to make many of the designs, and with a little bit of supervision, even children who are learning to knit can have a go at making a pair of bootees for their new brother or sister. Either follow the designs as they are or adapt them to suit your own colour choices, ribbons and embellishments to create a truly unique gift – with a little bit of love knitted into every stitch.
Happy knitting!

Hints and Tips

When knitting baby bootees, you will normally have a small number of stitches to cast on when beginning the project. It is therefore important to make sure the cast-on edge is elastic enough to enable the baby's foot to fit into the bootee when it is sewn up. Either cast on loosely, or use the thumb method of casting on that I have explained below.

Some of the designs in the book use the stranding method of colour work, in which the yarn not in use is stranded across the back of the work in the form of small loops. Always try to ensure that they are pulled reasonably taut; not so tight that they pucker the work, but tight enough to make sure that little toes do not get caught in them when putting on the bootees.

When sewing ribbons or embellishments on to bootees, make sure they are firmly attached so that the baby cannot pull them off. I have used no buttons as fastenings in any of the projects for this reason.

Increasing

m1 = make one stitch by picking up the strand between the stitch you are working and the next stitch on the needle, then knit into the back of it. This method of increasing is used where you do not want the increased stitch to be visible (see page 10).

Decreasing

K2togtbl = knit two stitches together through the back loops. This method of decreasing a stitch is used so that the stitch slants to the left (see page 10). It is normally worked with K2tog on the opposite side of the work to give a uniform look to the shaping.

Bobbles

Bobbles are used in knitting sometimes to create texture. They are made by knitting into the same stitch the stated number of times, then knitting one, two or even three rows on these stitches before finally decreasing the extra stitches to form the bobble. It is used in the pattern on page 20, where it is referred to as MB. A design will always state the required number of increases and decreases.

MB = make bobble as follows: K1, P1, K1 all into next st, turn, knit, turn, knit, slip 2nd and 3rd sts over 1st st (bobble made).

Making a twisted cord

1. Cut the yarn four times the length that you want your cord to be.
2. Making sure that your yarn is folded exactly in two, hold one end and ask someone else to hold the other end or loop it over something so that you can keep it taut.
3. Start twisting the yarn in one direction only until the whole length becomes tight and firm.

4. Stop twisting. Keeping tension on the end of the cord you are holding, reach for the centre and bring the two ends together.

5. Let go of the centre and allow your cord to twist on itself. Tie these two new ends together. Trim if required to form tiny tassels.

Using a blunt-ended needle

Almost all of the bootees in this book have ties of one kind or another. It is relatively easy to thread ribbon through eyelet holes, but where you need to thread through the actual knitted fabric a large-eyed, blunt-ended needle is very helpful. It allows you to push the cord or ribbon through between the stitches without catching or damaging the knitted fabric. In the same way, where little bits of embroidery are needed to embellish the bootees, a blunt-ended needle is far easier to use than a pointed one, and eliminates the danger of splitting or catching the knitted stitches while you are working.

Making a pompom

1. Cut two identical circles of cardboard. The diameter depends on the size of the pompom to be made and should be equal to the size of the finished pompom plus a little extra to allow you to trim it if needed. Cut a round hole in the centre of each circle to form a ring; the size of the hole should be approximately a quarter of the size of the finished pompom.

2. Holding the two rings of cardboard together, wind the wool evenly and tightly round and round, passing each winding through the hole in the middle and over the outer edge of the cardboard ring, until the hole is completely filled up with yarn.

3. Carefully cut through the yarn at the outer edge of the cardboard rings, making sure that the ball of yarn remains intact.

4. Take a piece of matching yarn, pass it between the two cardboard rings and tie it tightly around the centre of the wound yarn. As you pull tightly, the wound yarn will form into a round pompom. Tie a few tight knots to hold the pompom firmly in place.

5. Fluff up the pompom and trim the ends if needed.

Thumb method of casting on

This method of casting on gives a more elastic edge to the knitting. If you are left-handed, change 'right' and 'left' to 'left' and 'right' respectively.

1. Unwind sufficient yarn from the main ball to enable you to cast on the required number of stitches. Wind the yarn twice around the thumb of your left hand, leaving a long enough tail for the cast-on row, and form a slip knot on the needle. This is the first stitch.

2. Holding the needle and the tail-end of the yarn in your right hand, use your left hand to wrap the ball-end of the yarn clockwise around your left thumb, holding the yarn firmly.

3. Insert the tip of the needle up through the loop, wrap the yarn in your right hand around the back of the needle and draw it through the loop to form a stitch.

4. Continue in this way until you have the required number of stitches.

Sizing

All the bootees are designed to be worn by babies from birth to 1 year.

Daisy Chain

Materials:

1 x 50g ball 4-ply cashmere baby yarn in cream

50cm (20in) of flower braiding

50cm (20in) of deep pink baby ribbon

Needles:

1 pair 3.75mm (UK 9; US 5) knitting needles

Instructions:

Make two.

Using cream yarn, cast on 37 sts.

Row 1: knit.

Row 2: K1, *inc in next st, K15, inc in next st*, K1, rep from * to * once, K1.

Row 3: knit.

Row 4: K2, *inc in next st, K15, inc in next st*, K3, rep from * to * once, K2.

Row 5: knit.

Row 6: K3, * inc in next st, K15, inc in next st*, K5, rep from * to * once, K3.

Row 7: knit.

Row 8: K4, *inc in next st, K15, inc in next st*, K7, rep from * to * once, K4.

Row 9: knit.

Row 10: K5, *inc in next st, K15, inc in next st*, K9, rep from * to * once, K5.

Row 11: knit.

Rows 12–29: beg with a knit row, cont in SS for 18 rows, ending with a purl row.

Row 30: K33, sl1, K1, psso, turn.

Row 31: sl1, K9, P2tog, turn.

Row 32: sl1, K9, sl1, K1, psso, turn.

Rows 33–48: rep rows 31 and 32 eight times.

Row 49: rep row 31.

Row 50: knit.

Rows 51–53: GS.

Make eyelet holes for the ribbon as follows:

Row 54: K1, *yfwd, K2tog*, rep from * to * to end.

Row 55: knit.

Work a further 24 rows in GS. Cast off.

To make up the bootees

Work in all the yarn ends. Cut the braiding into two equal lengths. Sew a piece of braid along the centre of the stocking-stitch panel on the side of each bootee. Sew up the foot and back seam neatly. Turn over the garter-stitch top to form a cuff. Cut the ribbon in half, thread it through the holes at the ankle (see page 7) and tie in a pretty bow.

Tiny Trainers

Materials:
1 x 50g ball DK baby yarn in denim blue
Oddment of DK baby yarn in bright red
Oddment of 4-ply yarn in dark blue for laces

Needles:
1 pair 3.75mm (UK 9; US 5) knitting needles

Instructions:

Make two.
Using denim blue yarn, cast on 27 sts.
Row 1: knit.
Row 2: K2, m1, K11, m1, K1, m1, K11, m1, K2 [31 sts].
Row 3: knit.
Row 4 : K2, m1, K12, m1, K3, m1, K12, m1, K2.
Row 5: knit.
Row 6: K2, m1, K13, m1, K5, m1, K13, m1, K2.
Row 7: knit.
Row 8: K2, m1, K14, m1, K7, m1, K14, m1, K2.
Row 9: knit.

To form the red edging around the base of the bootee:
Rows 10–15: join in bright red yarn and work 6 rows in SS.
Break red and rejoin denim blue yarn.
Rows 16–25: work 10 rows in GS.
Rows 26–27: join in red yarn and work 2 rows in GS.
Break red and cont in denim blue.
Shape instep as follows:
Row 28: K26, turn.
Row 29: K9, turn.
Row 30: K8, K2tog, turn.
Row 31: K8, K2togtbl, turn.
Rows 32–41: rep rows 30 and 31 five times, turn.
Row 42: K9, knit across rem sts on LH needle.
Row 43: knit across all sts.
Rows 44–61: work 18 rows in GS.
Break denim blue yarn and join in bright red yarn.
Rows 62–65: work 4 rows in GS. Cast off.

To make up the bootees
Work in all the yarn ends. Working from the wrong side, sew the red edging by catching together, stitch by stitch, the 6 rows of SS at the base of each bootee. This will form a neat ridge on the right side of the work. Sew the seam on the base of the foot and then join the leg seam, matching the rows. Work lacing up the front of the bootees using a large-eyed, blunt-ended needle (see page 7), as you would on a real boot.

Pompom Bootees

Materials:

1 x 50g ball DK baby yarn in green fleck

Needles:

1 pair 3.75mm (UK 9; US 5) knitting needles

2 stitch holders

Instructions:

Make two.

Cast on 29 sts using the thumb method (see page 7).

Rows 1–4: GS.

Row 5: (RS facing) P2, *K1, P2*, rep from * to * to end.

Row 6: K2, *P1, K2*, rep from * to * to end.

Rows 7–28: rep rows 5 and 6 eleven times.

Row 29: knit.

Row 30: purl.

Divide for instep as follows:

Row 31: K9, (P2, K1) 3 times, P2, turn and slip rem 9 sts on to a stitch holder.

Row 32: K2, (P1, K2) 3 times, slip rem 9 sts on to second stitch holder.

Row 33: (P2, K1) 3 times, P2.

Row 34: K2, (P1, K2) 3 times.

Rows 35–50: working on these 11 sts, rep rows 33 and 34 eight times.

Break yarn.

Slip 9 sts from second holder on to the free needle with point at inner end, rejoin yarn and pick up and knit 11 sts along first side of instep. Knit across 11 sts on needle, pick up and knit 11 sts down other side of instep then knit across 9 sts from first stitch holder [51 sts].

Work in GS on these sts for 11 rows.

Shape foot as follows:

Next row: K2tog, K17, K2tog, K9, K2tog, K17, K2tog.

Next row: knit.

Next row: K2tog, K15, K2tog, K9, K2tog, K15, K2tog.

Next row: knit.

Cast off.

To make up the bootees

Work in the ends carefully. Join the leg and underfoot seams neatly. Fold over the top of each bootee to form a cuff. Make two small pompoms (see page 7). Trim them to a neat shape and sew one to the front of each bootee.

12

Baby Snugs

Materials:

1 x 50g ball 4-ply cashmere baby yarn in beige

Oddment of white eyelash yarn

Needles:

1 pair 3.75mm (UK 9; US 5) knitting needles

Instructions:

Make two.

Using beige yarn, cast on 33 sts.

Row 1: knit.

Row 2: K2, m1, K14, m1, K1, m1, K14, m1, K2.

Row 3: knit.

Row 4: K2, m1, K16, m1, K1, m1, K16, m1, K2.

Row 5: knit.

Row 6: K2, m1, K18, m1, K1, m1, K18, m1, K2.

Row 7: knit.

Continue to inc in this way until 53 sts on needle.

Join in white eyelash yarn and knit 2 rows.

Break contrast, continue in beige wool and SS for 2 rows.

Shape instep as follows:

Next row: K24, K2tog, K1, sl1, K1, psso, K24.

Next row: purl.

Next row: K23, K2tog, K1, K2togtbl, K23.

Next row: purl.

Continue to dec in this way until 37 sts remain, ending on a purl row.

Work 6 rows in SS. Break beige wool and join in eyelash yarn.

Work 2 rows in GS, cast off.

Side trims
Make two.

Using white eyelash yarn, cast on 10 sts.

Work 4 rows in GS, cast off.

To make up the bootees

Work in the ends and sew up the foot and back seams of the bootees. Sew on a side trim, using the picture as a guide. Using beige wool, make two twisted cords, approximately 20–25cm (8–10in) long, and four tiny pompoms (see pages 6–7). Use a large-eyed, blunt-ended needle to thread the cord in and out of the knitted fabric just below the last two rows of eyelash yarn. Attach a tiny pompom firmly to each end of the twisted cord.

Moon Boots

Materials:

1 x 50g ball DK eyelash yarn in blue/green mix
1 x 50g ball DK yarn in white

Needles:

1 pair 3.75mm (UK 9; US 5) knitting needles
2 stitch holders

Instructions:

Make two.

Using eyelash yarn, cast on 29 sts using the thumb method (see page 7).
Rows 1–10: GS. Break eyelash yarn.
Change to white DK.
Row 11: (RS facing) P2, *K1, P2*, rep from * to * to end.
Row 12: K2, *P1, K2 *, rep from * to * to end.
Rows 13–28: rep rows 11 and 12 eight times.
Row 29: knit.
Row 30: purl.
Divide for instep as follows:
Row 31: K9, (P2, K1) 3 times, P2, turn and slip rem 9 sts on to a stitch holder.
Row 32: K2, (P1, K2) 3 times, slip rem 9 sts on to second holder.
Row 33: (P2, K1) 3 times, P2.
Row 34: K2, (P1, K2) 3 times [11 sts].
Working on these 11 sts, rep the last 2 rows eight times more.
Break yarn.

Slip 9 sts from holder 2 on to the free needle with point at inner end, rejoin yarn and pick up and knit 11 sts along first side of instep.
Knit across 11 sts on needle, pick up and knit 11 sts down other side of instep then knit across 9 sts from holder 1 [51 sts].
Next row: knit.
Break white yarn and join in eyelash yarn.
Work 10 rows in GS.
Shape foot as follows:
Next row: K2tog, K17, K2tog, K9, K2tog, K17, K2tog.
Next row: knit.
Next row: K2tog, K15, K2tog, K9, K2tog, K15, K2tog.
Next row: knit.
Cast off.

To make up the bootees

Work in the ends carefully. Join the leg and underfoot seams neatly. Fold over the eyelash-yarn top to form a cuff at the top of each bootee.

Simply Blue

Materials:

1 x 50g ball 4-ply baby yarn in blue

Needles:

1 pair 3.75mm (UK 9; US 5) knitting needles

Instructions:

Make two.
Cast on 37 sts.
Row 1: knit.
Row 2: K1, *inc in next st, K15, inc in next st, K1*, rep from * to *.
Row 3: knit.
Row 4: K2, *inc in next st, K15, inc in next st*, K3, rep from * to *, K2.
Row 5: knit.
Row 6: K3, *inc in next st, K15, inc in next st*, K5, rep from * to *, K3.
Row 7: knit.
Row 8: K4, *inc in next st, K15, inc in next st,* K7, rep from * to *, K4.
Row 9: knit.
Row 10: K5, *inc in next st, K15, inc in next st*, K9, rep from * to *, K5.
Row 11: knit.
Work ridge pattern as follows:
Row 12: knit.
Row 13: purl.
Row 14: knit.
Row 15: knit.
Row 16: purl.
Row 17: knit.

Rep rows 12–17 once.
Shape instep as follows:
Row 1: K33, sl1, K1, psso, turn.
Row 2: sl1, K9, P2tog, turn.
Row 3: sl1, K9, sl1, K1, psso, turn.
Rep rows 2 and 3 eight times.
Rep row 2.
Next row: knit.
Work 3 more rows in GS, decreasing 1 st in centre of last row.
Work twisted rib as follows:
Next row: *K1tbl, P1*, rep from * to *.
Rep row 1 twenty times, cast off in rib.

To make up the bootees
Sew up the foot and back seams neatly. Turn over the ribbed top to form a cuff.

So Sweet

Materials:
1 x 50g ball DK baby yarn in multi shade
1m (40in) of narrow baby ribbon in pink

Needles:
1 pair 3.75mm (UK 9; US 5) knitting needles

Instructions:

Make two.
Note: MB = make bobble (see page 6).

Cast on 33 sts.
Row 1: knit.
Row 2: K2, m1, K14, m1, K1, m1, K14, m1, K2.
Row 3: knit.
Row 4: K2, m1, K16, m1, K1, m1, K16, m1, K2.
Row 5: knit.
Row 6: K2, m1, K18, m1, K1, m1, K18, m1, K2.
Row 7: knit.
Continue to inc in this way until 53 sts
on needle.
Next row: purl.
Work a bobble row as follows:
(K4, MB) to last 3 sts, K3.
Next row: purl.
Work 2 rows in SS.
Shape instep as follows:
Next row: K24, K2tog, K1, K2togtbl, K24.
Next row: purl.
Next row: K23, K2tog, K1, K2togtbl, K23.
Next row: purl.
Continue to dec in this way until 37 sts rem,
ending on a purl row.
Work 4 rows in SS.

Work a bobble row as follows:
K3, *MB, K4*, rep from * to * to last 4 sts,
MB, K3.
Next row: purl.
Work 4 rows in GS, cast off.

To make up the bootees
Sew in the ends neatly. Sew up the foot and
back seams. Cut the ribbon in half then, using
a large-eyed, blunt-ended needle, thread the
ribbon through the knitting at the top of each
bootee just below the bobble row. Tie the
ribbon in a neat bow.

Pretty in Pink

Materials:

1 x 50g ball 4-ply baby yarn in bright pink
2 pink ribbon roses

Needles:

1 pair 3.75mm (UK 9; US 5) knitting needles

Instructions:

Right bootee

Cast on 48 sts.
Row 1: knit.
Row 2: (K2, m1, K1) twice, knit to last 6 sts, (K1, m1, K2) twice.
Row 3: knit.
Rows 4–5: rep rows 2 and 3 [56 sts].
Rows 6–7: knit.
Row 8: K25, (K1, m1) 6 times, knit to end [62 sts].
Rows 9–12: knit for 4 rows.
Rows 13–20: SS for 8 rows, beg with a knit row.
Shape foot as follows:
Row 21: K19, (K2tog) 12 times, knit to end [50 sts].

Row 22: P33, turn.
Row 23: (K2tog) 8 times, K1, turn.
Row 24: P10, turn.
Row 25: (K2tog) 5 times, K3, turn.
Cast off 11 sts, K to end. **
Work the ankle band as follows:
Next row: K13.
Next row: cast on 20 sts, knit to end.
Work the eyelet row as follows:
Knit to last 4 sts, yfwd, K2tog, K2.
Next 2 rows: knit.
Cast off.
Rejoin yarn to rem 13 sts and work 5 rows in GS, cast off.

Left bootee

Work as for right bootee to **.
Work the ankle band as follows:
Next row: K13.
Work 5 rows in GS, cast off.
Rejoin yarn to rem 13 sts, cast on 20 sts, knit to end.
Next row: knit.
Work the eyelet row as follows:
K2, K2tog, yfwd, knit to end.
Next 2 rows: knit.
Cast off.

To make up the bootees

Work in all the ends neatly. Using flat seams, join the underfoot, heel and back seams. Sew a ribbon rose to the front of each shoe (make sure they are very secure to eliminate any danger of the baby pulling them off). Make two twisted cords, each approximately 20–25cm (8–10in) long (see page 6). Take one cord and use a large-eyed, blunt-ended needle to thread it through a stitch on the ankle band, on the outer side of the shoe. To position the cord, fold the ankle band over the baby's foot and align it with the eyelet hole. Tie the cord in a small knot to secure, leaving two ends of equal length. Fold the ankle band over the front of the shoe and thread the cord through the eyelet hole. Tie it in a bow.

Baby Boy Stripes

Materials:

1 x 50g ball DK baby yarn in brown
Oddments of DK baby yarn in blue and green

Needles:

1 pair 3.75mm (UK 9; US 5) knitting needles

Instructions:

Make two.

Using brown yarn, cast on 27 sts.
Row 1: knit.
Row 2: K2, m1, K11, m1, K1, m1, K11, m1, K2 [31sts].
Row 3: knit.
Row 4: K2, m1, K12, m1, K3, m1, K12, m1, K2 [35 sts].

Row 5: knit.
Row 6: K2, m1, K13, m1, K5, m1, K13, m1, K2 [39 sts].
Row 7: knit.
Row 8: K2, m1, K14, m1, K7, m1, K14, m1, K2 [43 sts].
Row 9: knit.
Rows 10–15: join in blue yarn and work 6 rows in SS. (These rows, when stitched together on the wrong side of the work, form the small ridge around the bootee foot.)
Join in brown and green and work in GS.
Rows 16–17: knit in brown.
Rows 18–19: knit in green.
Rows 20–21: knit in blue.
Rows 22–27: rep rows 16–21.
Rows 28–29: knit in brown.
Continue in brown and shape instep as follows:
Row 30: K26, turn.
Row 31: K9, turn.
Row 32: K8, K2tog, turn.
Row 33: K8, K2togtbl, turn.
Rows 34–43: rep rows 32–33 five times, turn.
Row 44: K9, knit across rem sts on left-hand needle.
Row 45: knit across all sts.
Rows 46–47: GS.
Row 48: make eyelet holes. K2, *yfwd, K2tog, K1*, rep from * to * to last 2 sts, yfwd, K2tog.
Row 49: purl.
Work 20 rows in K1, P1 rib.
Break brown yarn and join in blue yarn.
Work 2 rows in K1, P1 rib.
Break blue yarn and join in green yarn.
Work 2 rows in K1, P1 rib, cast off in rib.

To make up the bootees

Work in all the ends neatly. Sew up the foot and back seam, matching the stripes as you do so. Turn down the ribbing to form the cuff on each bootee. Make two twisted cords approximately 20–25cm (8–10in) long using two lengths of contrasting yarn (see page 6). Thread through the holes at the ankle using a large-eyed, blunt-ended needle (see page 7) and tie in a bow.

Bumble Bee Boots

Materials:

1 x 50g ball 4-ply baby yarn in black

1 x 50g ball 4-ply baby yarn in yellow

Oddment of 4-ply baby yarn in white

Needles:

1 pair 3.75mm (UK 9; US 5) knitting needles

Crochet hook

Instructions:

Make two.

Using black yarn, cast on 37 sts.

Rows 1–3: GS.

Join in yellow yarn and work the stripes in SS.

Rows 4–7: SS in yellow.

Rows 8–9: SS in black.

Rows 10–15: rep rows 4–9.

Rows 16–19: rep rows 4–7.

Break yellow.

Shape instep as follows:

Row 20: using black yarn, K24, turn.

Row 21: P11, turn.

Rows 22–25: join in yellow yarn and work 4 rows in SS.

Rows 26–27: join in black yarn and work 2 rows in SS.

Rows 28–31: join in yellow yarn and work 4 rows in SS.

Break yellow and continue in black only.

Rows 32–37: GS.

Break black.

Shape foot as follows:

With right-side facing, rejoin black yarn and pick up and knit 10 sts along first side of instep, 11 sts from instep, 10 sts along other side of instep, and knit across rem 13 sts [57 sts].

Work 15 rows in GS.

Next row: K1, *K2togtbl, K23, K2tog, K1*, rep from * to * to end of row.

Next row: knit.

Next row: K1, *K2togtbl, K21, K2tog, K1*, rep from * to * to end of row.

Next row: knit.

Next row: K1, *K2togtbl, K19, K2tog, K1*, rep from * to * to end of row.

Next row: knit.

Cast off.

To make up the bootees

Work in all the ends neatly. Join the foot and leg seams, matching the stripes as you do so. Using black yarn, make two pairs of antennae. For each pair, make a knitted cord by casting on 24 sts, then casting off. Work in the ends. Using a crochet hook, pull each end of one knitted cord through to the front of a bootee, positioning them as shown in the picture, and secure the cord in the centre on the inside of the bootee. Curl each end of the antennae into a tiny ball and secure with a few stitches. Embroider the eyes and mouth using white and black yarn, using the picture for guidance.

Spring Flowers

Materials:

1 x 50g ball Quick Knit baby yarn in white

Oddments of 4-ply baby yarn in lemon and green

1m (40in) narrow baby ribbon in white

Needles:

1 pair 3.75mm (UK 9; US 5) knitting needles

Instructions:

Make two.

Using white yarn, cast on 33 sts.

Rows 1–3: GS.

Work pattern as follows:

Row 4: (K3, P3) 5 times, K3.

Row 5: (P3, K3) 5 times, P3.

Rows 6–7: rep rows 4 and 5.

Row 8: (K3, P3) 5 times, K3.

Row 9: (P3, K3) 5 times, P3.

Rows 10–11: rep rows 8 and 9.

Rows 12–19: rep rows 4–11.

Row 20: K1, *yfwd, K2tog*, rep from * to * to end of row.

Row 21: purl.

Row 22: K23, turn.

Row 23: P13, turn and work on these sts for the instep.

Row 24: P2, K3, P3, K3, P2.

Row 25: K2, P3, K3, P3, K2.

Rows 26–27: rep rows 24–25.

Row 28: K2, P3, K3, P3, K2.

Row 29: P2, K3, P3, K3, P2.

Rows 30–31: rep rows 28 and 29.

Rows 32–35: work rows 4–7 again.

Break yarn and rejoin to inside edge of 10 sts. Pick up and knit these 10 sts, then pick up and knit 10 sts from first side of instep, 13 sts from instep, 10 sts along other side of instep, and finally knit across 10 sts on left-hand needle [53 sts].

Work 11 rows in GS.

Shape foot as follows:

Next row: *K1, K2tog, K21, K2tog*, rep from * to * once, K1.

Next row: K1, K2tog, knit to last 3 sts, K2tog, K1.

Next row: *K1, K2tog, K18, K2tog*, rep from * to * once, K1.

Next row: K1, K2tog, knit to last 3 sts, K2tog, K1.

Cast off.

To make up the bootees

Using the blunt-ended needle and lemon yarn, work tiny flowers using lazy daisy stitch randomly on the checkered top of the bootee. Using green yarn, embroider two tiny leaves beside each of the flowers. Work in the ends neatly. Join the foot and back seams. Thread ribbon through the eyelet holes at the ankles (see page 7) and tie in a pretty bow.

Fairy Slippers

Materials:

1 x 50g ball 4-ply cashmere baby yarn in lilac
1 x 50g ball 4-ply cashmere baby yarn in yellow

Needles:

1 pair 3.75mm (UK 9; US 5) knitting needles

Instructions:

Make two.
Using lilac yarn, cast on 33 sts.
Row 1: knit.
Row 2: K2, m1, K14, m1, K1, m1, K14, m1, K2.
Row 3: knit.
Row 4: K2, m1, K16, m1, K1, m1, K16, m1, K2.
Row 5: knit.
Row 6: K2, m1, K18, m1, K1, m1, K18, m1, K2.
Row 7: knit.
Continue to inc in this way until 53 sts
on needle.
Join in yellow yarn.
Work 2 rows in SS.
Change to lilac yarn.
Next row: K24, K2tog, K1, sl1,
K1, psso, K24.
Next row: knit.
Change to yellow yarn.
Next row: K23, K2tog, K1, K2togtbl, K23.
Next row: purl.
Change to lilac yarn.
Next row: K22, K2tog, K1, K2togtbl, K22.
Next row: knit.
Change to yellow.

Next row: K21, K2tog, K1, K2togtbl, K21.
Next row: purl.
Continue decreasing in this way, working 1 st
less at both ends of each row and maintaining
striped pattern, until 37 sts remain.
Work 4 more rows in striped pattern.
Change to yellow yarn and make eyelet holes
as follows.
Next row: K1, *yfwd, K2tog*, rep from * to *
to end of row.
Next row: purl.
Break yellow and continue in lilac.
Work 8 rows in GS.
Cast off.

To make up the bootees

Work in all the ends neatly. Join the foot and
back seams, matching the stripes as you do so.
Make two twisted cords approximately 20–25cm
(8–10in) long using yellow yarn (see page 6) and
thread them through the holes at the top of
each bootee using a large-eyed, blunt-ended
needle (see page 7). Tie in a bow.

Roses and Violets

Materials:

1 x 50g ball 4-ply baby yarn in lilac
1 x 50g ball 4-ply baby yarn in pink
1m (40in) of matching pink baby ribbon

Needles:

1 pair 3.75mm (UK 9; US 5) knitting needles

Instructions:

Right bootee

Using lilac yarn, cast on 48 sts.
Row 1: knit.
Row 2: (K2, m1, K1) twice, knit to last 6 sts, (K1, m1, K2) twice.
Row 3: knit.
Rows 4–5: rep rows 2 and 3 [56 sts].
Rows 6–7: knit.
Row 8: K25, (K1, m1) 6 times, knit to end of row [62 sts].
Row 9: purl.
Join in pink and work in pattern as follows:
Row 10: K2 lilac, K1 pink, *K3 lilac, K1 pink*, rep from * to * to last 3 sts, K3 lilac.

Rows 11–13: SS in lilac.
Row 14: K4 lilac, *K1 pink, K3 lilac*, rep from * to * to last 2 sts, K2 lilac.
Rows 15–17: SS in lilac.
Row 18: rep row 10.
Rows 19–20: SS in lilac.
Break lilac.
Row 21: purl in pink.
Row 22: K19, (K2tog) 12 times, knit to end of row [50 sts].
Row 23: P33, turn.
Row 24: (K2tog) 8 times, K1, turn.
Row 25: P10, turn.
Row 26: (K2tog) 5 times, K3, turn.
Cast off 11 sts, knit to end. **
Work the ankle band as follows:
Next row: K13.
Next row: cast on 20 sts, knit to end.
Work the eyelet row as follows:
Knit to last 4 sts, yfwd, K2tog, K2.
Next 2 rows: knit.
Cast off.
Rejoin yarn to rem 13 sts and work 5 rows in GS.
Cast off.

Left bootee

Work as for right bootee to **.
Work the ankle band as follows:
Next row: K13.
Work 5 rows in GS.
Cast off.
Rejoin yarn to rem 13 sts, cast on 20 sts, knit to end.
Next row: knit.
Work the eyelet row as follows:
K2, K2tog, yfwd, knit to end.
Next 2 rows: knit.
Cast off.

Flowers

Make one pink and one lilac flower for each bootee.
Cast on 18 sts.
Row 1: knit.
Row 2: knit twice into each st across row.
Cast off.

To make up the bootees

Work in all the ends neatly. Using flat seams, join the underfoot, heel and back seams. Sew two flowers on to the front of each bootee (make sure they are very secure to eliminate any danger of the baby pulling them off). Cut the ribbon into two equal pieces. Take one ribbon and use a large-eyed, blunt-ended needle to thread it through a stitch on the ankle band, on the outer side of the shoe. To position the ribbon, fold the ankle band over the baby's foot and align it with the eyelet hole. Secure the ribbon with small stitches, leaving two ends of equal length. Fold the band over the front of the shoe and thread the ribbon through the eyelet hole. Tie in a bow.

Candy Pink Toes

Materials:

1 x 50g ball 4-ply baby yarn in pink
Oddment of 4-ply baby yarn in white
50cm (20in) of pretty pink baby ribbon

Needles:

1 pair 3.75mm (UK 9; US 5) knitting needles

Instructions:

Make two.

Using pink yarn, cast on 37 sts.
Row 1: knit.
Row 2: K1, *inc in next st, K15, inc in next st, K1*, rep from * to * once.
Row 3: knit.
Row 4: K2, *inc in next st, K15, inc in next st*, K3, rep from * to * once, K2.
Row 5: knit.
Row 6: K3, *inc in next st, K15, inc in next st*, K5, rep from * to * once, K3.
Row 7: knit.
Row 8: K4, *inc in next st, K15, inc in next st*, K7, rep from * to * once, K4.
Row 9: knit.

Row 10: K5, *inc in next st, K15, inc in next st*, K9, rep from * to * once, K5.
Row 11: knit.
Join in white and work in two-colour pattern as follows:
Row 12: knit in pink.
Row 13: purl in pink.
Row 14: using white K1, *sl1, K1*, rep from * to * to end of row.
Row 15: rep row 14.
Row 16: knit in white.
Row 17: purl in white.
Row 18: using pink, K2, *sl1, K1*, rep from * to * to last 2 sts, K2.
Row 19: using pink, P1, K1, *sl1, K1*, rep from * to * to last st, P1.
Rows 20–27: rep rows 12 to 19.
Rows 28–29: GS in white.
Break white and continue in pink :
Row 30: K33, sl1, K1, psso, turn.
Row 31: sl1, K9, P2tog, turn.
Row 32: sl1, K9, sl1, K1, psso, turn.
Rows 33–48: rep rows 31 and 32 eight times.
Row 49: rep row 31.
Row 50: knit.
Rows 51–53: GS.
Make eyelet holes as follows.
Row 54: K1, *yfwd, K2tog*, rep from * to * to end of row.
Rows 55–57: GS, decreasing 1 st in centre of last row.
Work 20 rows in K2, P2 rib.
Cast off in rib.

To make up the bootees

Sew up the foot and back seams neatly. Turn over the ribbed top to form a cuff. Cut the ribbon in half and thread one half through the holes at the ankle of each bootee using a large-eyed, blunt-ended needle (see page 7). Tie in a pretty bow.

Little Blue Shoes

Materials:

1 x 50g ball DK baby yarn in royal blue
1 x 50g ball DK baby yarn in sparkly white

Needles:

1 pair 3.75mm (UK 9; US 5) knitting needles

Instructions:

Make two.

Using royal blue yarn, cast on 27 sts.
Row 1: knit.
Row 2: K2, m1, K11, m1, K1, m1, K11, m1,
K2 [31 sts].
Row 3: knit.
Row 4: K2, m1, K12, m1, K3, m1, K12, m1, K2.
Row 5: knit.
Row 6: K2, m1, K13, m1, K5, m1, K13, m1, K2.
Row 7: knit.
Row 8: K2, m1, K14, m1, K7, m1, K14, m1, K2.
Row 9: knit.
Rows 10–15: SS. (These rows, when stitched
together on the wrong side of the work, form
the small ridge around the bootee foot.)
Rows 16–28: GS.

Shape instep as follows:
Row 29: K26, turn.
Row 30: K9, turn.
Row 31: K8, K2tog, turn.
Row 32: K8, K2togtbl, turn.
Break royal blue yarn and join in sparkly white.
Continue in SS as follows:
Row 33: K8, K2tog, turn.
Row 34: P8, P2togtbl, turn.
Rows 35–42: rep rows 33 and 34 four
times, turn.
Row 43: K9, knit across rem sts on left-
hand needle.
Row 44: purl across all sts.
Rows 45–60: continue in SS for 16 rows, ending
on a purl row.
Rows 61–64: work 4 rows in K1, P1 rib.
Change to royal blue.
Rows 65–66: work 2 rows in K1, P1 rib.

Cast off in rib.

Bow

Make two.
Using sparkly white yarn, cast on 5 sts.
Rows 1–2: GS.
Rows 3–4: join in royal blue yarn and work 2
rows in GS.
Rows 5–12: rep rows 1–4 twice.
Rows 13–14: rep rows 1 and 2.
Cast off.

Strap

Make two.
Using royal blue yarn, cast on 4 sts.
Work 38 rows in GS.

Cast off.

To make up the bootees

Work in all the ends neatly. With wrong sides
facing, sew rows 10–15 together, matching
them stitch for stitch, to form a ridge on the
outside of the work. Sew the foot and back
seams neatly. Run a thread through the centre
blue stripe of each bow and draw it up to
gather the piece of knitting into a bow shape.
Secure the thread at the back of the work. Sew
a bow to the centre of each strap. Sew the
straps across the bootees at the ankle, stitching
on each side of the foot.

Berry Bootees

Materials:

1 x 50g ball 4-ply baby yarn in green

1 x 50g ball 4-ply baby yarn in red

Oddments of 4-ply baby yarn in yellow
and white

Needles:

1 pair 3.75mm (UK 9; US 5) knitting needles

Instructions:

Make two.
Using green yarn, cast on 37 sts.
Rows 1–5: GS. Break green yarn.
Join in red.
Rows 6–9: SS.
Join in yellow.
Row 10: K4 red, K1 yellow, *K3 red, K1 yellow*,
rep from * to * to last 4 sts, K4 red.
Rows 11–15: using red, work 5 rows in SS, beg
with a purl row.
Row 16: K2 red, *K1 yellow, K3 red*, rep from *
to * to last 3 sts, K1 yellow, K2 red.
Rows 17–21: using red, work 5 rows in SS, beg

with a purl row.
Row 22: K4 red, K1 yellow, *K3 red, K1 yellow*,
rep from * to * to last 4 sts, K4 red.
Rows 23–25: using red, work 3 rows in SS, beg
with a purl row.
Join in green yarn.
Shape instep as follows:
Row 26: K13 green, K11 red.
Turn and work on these 11 sts for instep.
Row 27: purl in red.
Row 28: K3 red, K1 yellow, K3 red, K1 yellow,
K3 red.
Rows 29–33: using red, work 5 rows in SS, beg
with a purl row.
Row 34: K5 red, K1 yellow, K5 red.
Rows 35–39: using red, work 5 rows in SS, beg
with a purl row.
Row 40: K3 red, K1 yellow, K3 red, K1 yellow,
K3 red.
Row 41: purl in red.
Break red.
With right sides facing and using green yarn,
pick up and knit 10 sts along first side of instep,
11 sts from instep, 10 sts down other side of
instep, and knit across rem 13 sts [57 sts].
Work 15 rows in GS.
Shape foot as follows:
Next row: K1, * K2togtbl, K23, K2tog, K1*, rep
from * to * to end of row.
Next row: knit.
Next row: K1, * K2togtbl, K21, K2tog, K1*, rep
from * to * to end of row.
Next row: knit.
Next row: K1, *K2togtbl, K19, K2tog, K1*, rep
from * to * to end of row.
Next row: knit.
Cast off.

Strap

Make two.
Using green yarn, cast on 4 sts.
Work 36 rows in GS. Cast off.

Flowers

Make two.

Using white yarn, cast on 30 sts.

Row 1: K1, *cast off next 4 sts (1 st rem on needle), K1*, rep from * to * to end of row.

Break yarn and run through sts on needle. Draw up tight to form flower shape and secure with a few sts. With yellow yarn, embroider a few French knots in centre of flower.

To make up the bootees

Work in the ends neatly. Join the foot and back seams. Sew a flower to the centre of each strap. Sew a strap across the ankle of each bootee, securing them firmly on each side.

Baby Lace

Materials:

1 x 50g ball 4-ply baby yarn in turquoise
1 x 50g ball 4-ply baby yarn in white
1m (40in) of matching turquoise baby ribbon

Needles:

1 pair 3.75mm (UK 9; US 5) knitting needles

Instructions:

Make two.

Using turquoise yarn, cast on 37 sts.
Rows 1–3: GS.
Join in white and work pattern:
Row 4: K1, *(K2tog) twice, (yfwd, K1) 3 times, yfwd, (sl1, K1, psso) twice, K1*, rep from * to * to end of row.
Row 5: purl.
Rows 6–9: rep rows 4 and 5 twice.
Rows 10–13: knit in turquoise.
Rows 14–23: rep rows 4–13.
Break turquoise and continue in white.

Work eyelet row:
Row 24: K1, *yfwd, K2tog*, rep from * to * across row.
Row 25: purl.
Shape instep as follows:
Row 26: K24, turn.
Row 27: P11, turn.
Continue on these 11 sts and work 18 rows in SS. Break yarn.
With right sides facing, pick up and knit 10 sts along first side of instep, 11 sts from instep, 10 sts down other side of instep, and knit across rem 13 sts [57 sts].
Work 15 rows in GS.
Shape foot as follows:
Next row: K1, *K2togtbl, K23, K2tog, K1*, rep from * to * to end of row.
Next row: knit.
Next row: K1, *K2togtbl, K21, K2tog, K1*, rep from * to * to end of row.
Next row: knit.
Next row: K1, *K2togtbl, K19, K2tog, K1*, rep from * to * to end of row.
Next row: knit.
Cast off.

To make up the bootees

Work in the ends neatly. Join the foot and back seams, matching the pattern as you do so. Cut the ribbon into two equal lengths. Thread one length through the eyelet holes at the ankle of each bootee using a large-eyed, blunt-ended needle (see page 7) and tie in a pretty bow.

Lavender Rose

Materials:

1 x 50g ball 4-ply baby yarn in white

1 x 50g ball 4-ply baby yarn in lavender

40cm (16in) of narrow (7mm) baby ribbon in
very pale lavender

40cm (16in) of narrow (3mm) baby ribbon
in lavender

2 lavender ribbon roses

Needles:

1 pair 3.75mm (UK 9; US 5) knitting needles

Instructions:

Make two.

Using white yarn, cast on 48 sts.

Work pattern as follows:

Row 1: knit.

Row 2: (K2, m1, K1) twice, knit to last 6 sts, (K1,
m1, K2) twice.

Row 3: knit.

Rows 4–5: rep rows 2 and 3 [56 sts].

Rows 6–7: knit.

Row 8: K25, (K1, m1) 6 times, knit to end of
row [62 sts].

Row 9: purl.

Join in lavender yarn and work picot edge
as follows:

Rows 10–13: SS.

Row 14: K1, *yfwd, K2tog*, rep from * to * to
last st, K1.

Row 15: purl.

Rows 16–19: SS. Break lavender and
rejoin white.

Rows 20–21: knit.

Rejoin lavender.

Row 22: K2 white, K1 lavender, *K3 white, K1
lavender,* rep from * to * to last 3 sts, K3 white.

Rows 23–25: SS in white.

Row 26: K4 white, *K1 lavender, K3 white*, rep
from * to * to last 2 sts, K2 white.

Rows 27–29: SS in white.

Row 30: rep row 22.

Rows 31–33: SS in white.

Shape top as follows:

Row 34: K19, (K2tog) 12 times, knit to end of
row [50 sts].

Row 35: P33, turn.

Row 36: (K2tog) 8 times, K1, turn.

Row 37: P10, turn.

Row 38: (K2tog) 5 times, K3, turn.

Cast off 11 sts, knit to end.

Ankle bands

Next row: knit 13.

Work 5 rows in GS.

Rejoin white yarn to rem 13 sts and work 6 rows
in GS.

Cast off.

To make up the bootees

Work in all the ends neatly. Working from the
wrong side of the bootee, sew the lavender
picot edge together (rows 10–19) matching
the seams stitch for stitch, thus forming a picot
border on the right side of each bootee. Using
a flat seam, join the underfoot, heel and back
seams. Cut each piece of ribbon into two
equal lengths and sew one length of each on
to the ends of the ankle bands. Tie them in
a pretty bow. Sew a ribbon rose firmly to the
toe of each bootee. Make sure they are firmly
attached so that the baby cannot pull them off.

A Pair of Ducklings

Materials:

1 x 50g ball of 4-ply baby yarn in yellow
Oddments of 4-ply yarn in orange and black
Tiny amount of stuffing for ducklings' heads

Needles:

1 pair 3.75mm (UK 9; US 5) knitting needles

Instructions:

Make two.
Using yellow yarn, cast on 48 sts.
Row 1: knit.
Row 2: (K2, m1, K1) twice, knit to last 6 sts, (K1, m1, K2) twice.
Row 3: knit.
Rows 4–5: rep rows 2 and 3 [56 sts].
Rows 6–7: knit.
Row 8: K25, (K1, m1) 6 times, knit to end of row [62 sts].
Work pattern as follows:
Row 9: (RS facing) (K1, P1) to end of row.
Row 10: knit.
Rows 11–24: rep rows 9 and 10 seven times.
Shape foot as follows:
Row 25: K19, (K2tog) 12 times, knit to end of row [50 sts].
Row 26: K33, turn.
Row 27: (K2tog) 8 times, K1, turn.
Row 28: K10, turn.

Row 29: (K2tog) 5 times, K3, turn.
Cast off 11 sts, knit to end.**

Top of bootee
Next row: knit 13 sts.
Next row: knit to last 2 sts, inc in next st, K1.
Next row: knit.
Rep last 2 rows until you have 18 sts on needle.
Work 6 rows in GS. Cast off.
Rejoin yarn to rem 13 sts and work other side of top to match, reversing incs.

Duckling head
Make two.
Using yellow yarn, cast on 10 sts.
Row 1: purl.
Row 2: inc in each st to end.
Row 3: purl.
Row 4: *K1, inc in next st*, rep from * to * to end of row.
Row 5: purl.
Rows 6–13: SS.
Row 14: *K1, K2tog*, rep from * to * to end of row.
Row 15: purl.
Row 16: K2tog across row.
Row 17: purl.
Row 18: K2tog across row. Break yarn and run through sts left on needle, draw up tightly and fasten off.

Beak
Make two.
Using orange yarn, cast on 7 sts.
Knit 1 row and cast off.

To make up the bootees
Work in all the ends neatly. Using flat seams, join the underfoot, heel and back seams. Turn the top back to form a cuff. Stitch the side seam of each duckling head, stuffing as you do so, forming each head into a neat little ball shape. Take a beak, work in the ends carefully, fold it in half lengthways and sew it to one of the heads. With black yarn, embroider tiny eyes either side of the beak. Make another head to match. Sew a head firmly to the front of each bootee. Make sure they are attached securely so that the baby cannot pull them off.

Rosie Toes

Materials:

1 x 50g ball of DK baby yarn in white

Oddment of DK baby yarn in pale pink

2 pink ribbon rose motifs

1m (40in) narrow pink baby ribbon

Needles:

1 pair 3.75mm (UK 9; US 5) knitting needles

Instructions:

Make two.

Using white yarn, cast on 27 sts.
Row 1: knit.
Row 2: K2, m1, K11, m1, K1, m1, K11, m1, K2 [31 sts].
Row 3: knit.
Row 4: K2, m1, K12, m1, K3, m1, K12, m1, K2.
Row 5: knit.
Row 6: K2, m1, K13, m1, K5, m1, K13, m1, K2.
Row 7: knit.
Row 8: K2, m1, K14, m1, K7, m1, K14, m1, K2.
Row 9: knit.

Join in pink yarn and work picot border as follows:
Rows 10–13: SS.
Row 14: K1, *yfwd, K2tog*, rep from * to * to end of row.
Row 15: purl.
Rows 16–17: knit.
Break pink and rejoin white.
Rows 18–29: GS.
Shape instep as follows:
Row 30: K26, turn.
Row 31: K9, turn.
Row 32: K8, K2tog, turn.
Row 33: K8, K2togtbl, turn.
Rows 34–43: rep rows 32 and 33 five times, turn.
Row 44: K9, knit across rem sts on left-hand needle.
Row 45: knit.
Work 18 rows in GS.
Break white and join in pink.
Work picot edging as follows:
Work 3 rows in SS.
Next row: K1, *yfwd, K2tog*, rep from * to * to end of row.
Next row: purl.
Work 4 rows in SS. Cast off loosely.

To make up the bootees

Work in all the yarn ends. Working with the wrong sides facing, sew up the pink picot edging by matching the sides together stitch by stitch. This will form a neat picot edge on the right side of the work. Sew the seam on the base of each foot and then join the leg seams, matching the rows. Fold over the pink picot edging at the top of each bootee on to the wrong side of the work and catch it down all around the inside. Cut the ribbon into two equal lengths and thread a length through the holes at each ankle (see page 7). Sew a ribbon rose motif firmly on to the toe of each bootee, so that the baby cannot pull them off.

Acknowledgements

Special thanks once again to Search Press
for their wonderful editorial skills, gorgeous
photography, and help and guidance in
putting this book together. Thanks also to
Sirdar for supplying me with the beautiful
yarns to knit all the projects. And last but
not least, a big thank you to my wonderful
friends and family for their never-ending
patience and encouragement while I was
writing this book.